Maat Publications

www.orderofthewhitelion.com (OWL)
www.isisqabalahtuition.com

Copyright © 2008 Jenni Shell & Lorraine Morgan

Production: Drew Westcott
www.drewwestcott.co.uk

All rights reserved.

ISBN: 1507630409
ISBN-13: 978-1507630402

YESOD

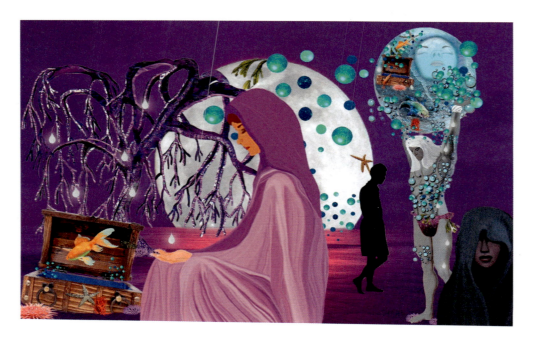

The Foundation

How to use this workbook

- ✦ Read through the Introduction to Qabalah and **how to visualise the Temple of Yesod**
- ✦ Practise building the imagery of Yesod Temple
- ✦ Read through the **Yesod Awareness** section and awareness meditation, and then repeat the meditation using memory as guidance
- ✦ Log any information received during awareness meditation
- ✦ Complete the awareness section before reading through Yesod Temple
- ✦ When familiar with the journey into the realms of Yesod – repeat using memory to guide you
- ✦ Get into the **Spirit of Yesod** – a practical experience
- ✦ Log everything you receive
- ✦ Consolidate

© Copyright Jenni Shell and Lorraine Morgan 2008 all rights reserved

These workbooks are compiled and written with the utmost integrity and concentration on correct procedures. However, it is essential that they are regarded as information only. In no event will the authors, or OWL/Isis websites, be liable for any consequences of the use of these workbooks, and therefore any action taken, or reliance placed on the information given, is entirely at your own risk.

Welcome

The Order of the White Lion and Isis Tuition are run by teachers who have completed an extensive study of spiritual awareness and in particular the Tree of Life, working very much on a practical level.

Our aim is to help raise awareness, not only of the teachings and how to use the Tree of Life, but also to help others find a way of living their lives more fully.

Yesod Index

3. Qabalah Introduction:
   - Spirit, Soul and Personality Working Together
6. Yesod – The Foundation
   - Description of the Temple of Yesod
9. Yesod Awareness
   - Yesod Awareness Meditation: **No Regrets**
17. The Power of the Subconscious

24. The Temple of Yesod
    - Temple of the Sea

30. Emotional Independence

31. State of the Subconscious

32. Acting on Intuition

33. Reincarnation

33. Astral Worlds and Spirit Guides
    - Personal Spirit Guides
37. Memory

38. The Spirit of Yesod

39. Experiencing Yesod

41. Yesod: Corresponding Information

42. **No Regrets** meditation record sheet

43. Yesod Consolidation

Qabalah Introduction

Qabalah is not a religion, it is a **Way of Life**.

The word **Qabalah** is a Hebrew word that means **to receive Inner Wisdom.**

Qabalah is a wealth of ancient knowledge that promotes a **Way of Life** achieved through **Inner Wisdom.**

This Way of Life has been passed on orally throughout the ages and is frequently known as the Kabbalah as it comes from Jewish origins.

Although the essence is the same the word Qabalah is often used by those of non-Jewish background linked to the western world.

According to Jewish tradition an archangel gave Adam the teachings - as he and Eve were expelled from the Garden of Eden - to help them, and their descendants, find their way back to the garden and Word of God.

It is believed the teachings were also given to Abraham, the father of the Jewish nation, to be used as a guide back to God, the spiritual source and the original plan.

These ancient teachings, handed down through the ages, are mapped out on the Tree of Life.

The Tree of Life is a tool that can be used on a daily basis.

Its implementation can be compared to using a roadmap in that it provides a solid structure for us to follow as we journey through life, exploring and discovering more about our Selves, our Purpose and the part we play in the Bigger Picture.

Spirit, Soul and Personality Working Together

Within the structure of the Tree of Life are three triangles.

If we look at a coloured picture of the Tree of Life, and start at the top, the first triangle: **white**, **grey** and **black** represents the spiritual part of us. For example, our **spiritual desire, direction** and **motive**. Those three circles or sephiroth also represent the **Bigger, Spiritual Picture** that affects the whole of humanity.

The second triangle: **blue**, **red** and **yellow** aligns with our **ideals, conscience, intuition** and individual **soul**. It also represents the **Soul level of Humanity**. This triangle is sandwiched in the middle and known as the ethical or moral triangle of the **Inner Plane** soul level.

The third triangle: **green**, **orange** and **violet** relates to our **feelings, thoughts** and **emotional reactions** and **responses**, and is representative of our individual **personalities**. It also represents the **Personality of Humanity**.

The **white** sephirah at the top of the Tree is called Kether. **Kether** represents Completion of the Great Work, and the return to the **Source of Creation**.

Malkuth at the bottom of the Tree represents our planet Earth, physical manifestation and the world of creation. On an individual level Malkuth aligns with our physical body, and the way we take action and behave. Here we explore the life we have created for ourselves.

The sephirah Malkuth is associated with the four colours: **ochre**, **olive**, **russet** and **black**.

* The colours shown are the archangel colours. The sephiroth also correspond with other colours associated with the Four Worlds.

These sephiroth are also known as **Temples** or inner **connection points**.

A temple is a place where we can make a very strong connection with our psyche that we may not be able to do in our everyday life.

Our psyche is our higher mind; the higher aspect of us.

The Temples are very different.

They are not places of worship.

They are places where we can make a connection. Somewhere we can go to meditate and contemplate on certain aspects within ourselves. We use these inner temples for information or guidance to help us on our journey through life.

In the Qabalah we have ten temples or places of connection, not only with our psyche (higher self) but also with universal forces; higher, more evolved spiritual beings, astral beings and other dimensions. We can also make and strengthen our connection with our own guides.

In the early stages it is advisable to find an area of privacy and quiet to make a connection without distraction but as we get more proficient we will find we can make a connection at any time, and anywhere.

Each temple offers a challenge to overcome and will reveal, and highlight, different aspects within ourselves, and our personalities. We all have these different aspects and traits. Some may be more pronounced than others.

Some may need to be brought out of the darkness.

The idea is to take the Qabalistic teachings and start by working our way up the Tree of Life. The Qabalah helps to raise awareness of ourselves, our environment and those around us. This is how we learn and how we transmute our karma.

As we travel on our journey of spiritual awareness we will be shown, and given information, and maybe challenged in our everyday life on how we **think**, **feel** and **react** in certain situations, and around certain people.

By making a connection with a temple we are drawing that influence towards us. Events may occur in our day to day life that need to be brought to our attention.

All of these temples exist in the astral worlds but we need to make them real for us. When we go into these temples we want to feel that we are really there, that we are **actually in them**, feeling them and smelling the aromas rather than just imagining we are.

Some people find building imagery up around them easier than others. We use our own imagery and go with whatever we get. We will get information that is relevant to us and us alone.

The journey into the temples and up the Tree of Life is one of experience and this experience is personal to you. Everyone's journey will be different and what works for you may not work for someone else.

Yesod – The Foundation

When studying the Tree of Life we often start at the bottom and familiarise ourselves first with sephirah number ten, the temple of **Earth**. The Hebrew name for this sephirah is **Malkuth**. It is also known as the **Kingdom**.

Malkuth represents the **physical plane** and gets us looking at how we handle the **energy** of the **material** world.

The way it works on a practical level within the Qabalah is to use the Tree of Life, the sephiroth and the paths, as a means of helping ourselves in our everyday lives.

Whatever is happening to us on a day to day level we can relate it to the Tree.

For example, if we are having problems keeping ourselves grounded or experiencing challenging issues around money we could look to the Temple of Malkuth to help us find answers.

If we are experiencing difficulties within relationships then we would look to another temple - the Temple of Netzach.

Yesod - sephirah number 9 - is directly above Malkuth on the Tree of Life and astrologically aligns with the **Moon**. Yesod focuses on the power of the **subconscious**, our **emotional foundation** and emotional **stability**. Yesod also links us to the **Astral Worlds** and **spirit guides**.

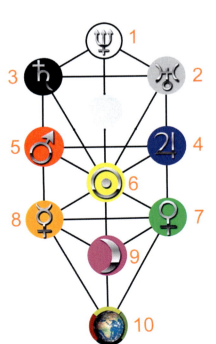

Each temple helps us in different areas of our lives, they are not all the same. The teachings of the Qabalah help to get us focused and aware of how we operate on all levels: physically, emotionally, mentally and so on.

The way the temples work for us is through the powers of visualisation and through our senses and feelings. The following is a basic exercise designed to aid the initial process of building the imagery around Yesod – the Temple of the Sea.

The images of all the Temples on the Tree of Life are already built in the ether and connecting into that energy which has been used by thousands of others over the years creates immense power.

For this reason the description has been kept simple. It is not wise to attempt any kind of temple or path-working without proper guidance and controls in place.

Description of the Temple of Yesod

This is an incredibly beautiful sea temple.

From the outside there is a crescent-shaped pool and a silver bridge that spans across it, leading to the temple of Yesod.

You have to cross the bridge to reach the temple.

The temple is pagoda shaped, exquisite in structure, cut in mother of pearl with turrets of silver.

Inside the temple and set in the walls are four silver doors with handles made of mother of pearl.

The door through which you enter the temple is one of the four doors.

The other three doors are situated at the far end behind the altar and lead onto other paths and temples.

The walls of the temple are made of thousands of silver mirrors, all different shapes and sizes, which arch over your head.

If you look up to the ceiling you will see a night sky and if you look at the mirrors without looking for yourself you will see billowing sea all around the temple.

You can also see your reflection in them; the mirrors will reflect back to you what you need to see and know.

The floor is made of silver and midnight blue tiles, which are warm to the touch.

Set in the floor, within each of the four corners of the temple in silver and ebony, are phases of the moon in different stages:

- ✦ The moon in the **East** (ahead of you) is a **new** moon

- ✦ In the **South** (on your right) is a **full** moon

- ✦ In the **West** (behind you) is a **waning** moon

- ✦ And in the **North** (on your left) it is a **dark** moon

Inside the temple there is also another, smaller, crescent-shaped pool spanned by a small bridge of mother of pearl and hanging overhead, as if suspended in space, are nine silver lamps.

In the centre of the temple is an altar made of white marble.

On top of the altar are nine silver goblets and a silver bowl with the blue flame of memory in it. The blue flame of memory is always alight.

Two pillars stand either side of the altar.

The pillar is on the right is mother of pearl and the pillar on the left is dark midnight blue.

The **Archangel** associated with Yesod is **Gabriel**.

Gabriel is often seen standing between the two pillars. He is exceedingly beautiful and very powerful. He radiates love and wears misty, swirling robes of violet blue and sea-green.

Gabriel is the archangel of love. Always swirling around him are the **Aishim** – the **angelic hosts**. The Aishim are the angels of Yesod. They are known as the souls of fire.

Gabriel may invite you to drink from the waters of life, the vital soul of existence from one of the silver goblets.

Later in the workbook there is a more in-depth awareness and meditation on the Sea Temple of Yesod.

Yesod Awareness

Yesod is sephirah number nine and situated directly above sephirah number ten (Malkuth) which is at the base of the Tree of Life.

Malkuth represents our physical body and the world we have created for ourselves on the material plane.

Malkuth is the Kingdom of the physical world and everything that we can perceive through our five senses has its roots here.

All Qabalistic work begins and ends with the sephirah Malkuth.

Malkuth leads you into all the other temples and paths and is the sephirah you always return to – to bring you back into the physical world and your physical surroundings.

Yesod, sephirah number nine, represents our **subconscious** and **emotional foundation**.

How emotionally stable we are, depends on how strong our emotional foundation is.

How emotionally stable do you consider yourself to be?

Do you find it easy to forgive and forget or do you bear grudges and feel hurt and resentful?

Are you easily hurt?

Life is a series of choices.

Sometimes we get it right, and sometimes we don't.

The Qabalah teaches us there are no rights or wrongs – we just have to go with what is right for us, and realise and learn from what is wrong for us.

What might be **right for us** though, could be very **wrong for others**.

The key is to recognise what isn't working in our life and learn from it rather than try to cling on.

What is your **attitude** towards **past events** in your life?

Do you **let go** of **anxieties** and past **regrets**?

We are not going to get far on our journey through life if we are going to spend our time clinging onto the past or regretting what may have been.

Rather than reliving memories of all that has gone before, try looking at what is happening in the **now** with **fresh** eyes and **attitudes**.

Don't drag **past experiences** into **current** situations.

Do you tend to do that?

The key is to **learn** from our **past mistakes** and try to ensure we don't repeat them in the future.

It is whether we do manage to prevent those mistakes from occurring again that determines whether we have learnt anything or not.

It's no good regretting after the event the way you handled something or someone – what's done is done.

So, don't waste time on regret.

Just learn from the experience and try not to repeat the same mistakes over, and over, again.

The following is a visualisation that focuses on one aspect of energy associated with the subconscious.

This is an introduction to the awareness of Yesod, the Temple of the Sea, and the sephirah where the subconscious is situated on The Tree of Life.

It is about understanding this energy, and learning how to let go of unfortunate memories that are no longer of value to us.

Before we can do this we need to contemplate deeply and take a long look at the worth and meaning of our possessions and our emotional reliance.

What do we try to hold on to in the name of **security**?

This meditation is most valuable when your eyes are closed and you visualise the experience as you go along.

If possible get someone to read it out to you. Then, if they too wish to participate, allow them to do the same as yourself, and discuss your experiences afterwards. It always helps to share things with another.

Before beginning any kind of spiritual or visualisation work it is worthwhile spending some time preparing for meditation – making sure you are sitting in a comfortable relaxed position either on the floor or in a chair with your back straight, this helps with the flow of energy.

Rest your hands in your lap and try to ensure you are not likely to be disturbed.

If you are not comfortable then you are likely to be distracted and not able to meditate.

Wrapping a blanket around you can also help with relaxation as well as keep you warm.

Breathe naturally and if you burn incense or use essential oils these can also help to relax you.

Following the same procedure each time you meditate helps to impress upon the subconscious that you are preparing to raise your vibrations to connect with your higher self; your intuition.

To help you prepare and clear your mind of outside influences there is a section on meditation and relaxation techniques on the OWL website you may find useful.

www.orderofthewhitelion.com

Yesod Awareness Meditation

To prepare:

Read the description first and then try to follow it from memory.

If possible, get someone to read it out slowly to you with sufficient pauses to allow you time to see the visualisation clearly. Then, if they too wish to participate, allow them to do the same as yourself, and discuss your experiences afterwards.

It always helps to share things with another.

- ✦ If you have read the information on the Owl website you will remember to sit in a comfortable, relaxed position – either on the floor or in a chair with your back straight. This helps with the flow of energy. Have your palms uppermost resting in your lap

- ✦ Breathe evenly and naturally

- ✦ You may wish to burn incense or use essential oils. These can help to relax you. Following the same procedure each time you meditate helps to impress upon the subconscious that you are preparing to raise your vibrations to connect with your higher self; your intuition

- ✦ Record any information received (see page 42)

No Regrets

Make yourself comfortable and relax.

Gently close your eyes and relax.

This, like all the visualisations is about you.

Only you.

Any judgements you make are judgements about you, and nobody else.

Any feelings you have belong only to you, and nobody else.

You may share your thoughts with others if you like, but the choice is always yours.

You have your own power. You are your own protector.

You can trust yourself.

So, make yourself comfortable and relax.

Concentrate all your attention on your body.

What language is it expressing at this moment?

If your legs or arms are crossed you are saying: **I'm very tense and need to protect myself**.

If your back is hunched it may seem, even to you, that you are carrying the weight of the world on your shoulders.

Why not let it go.

Let it go ....

Uncross your legs and arms. Straighten your back. You don't have to carry this stress with you right now.

Take a deep breath and let go. For as long as you are here, in this place, you have allowed yourself the time to let go of all restrictions. So make the most of that time.

Take a deep breath and let go.

Now feel the difference in your posture. Feel the tension relax. Take another deep breath and continue to breathe deeply for a moment. Full deep breaths.

Each breath allows you to relax more, and more.

Breathe in. Breathe out.

Spend just a moment now expanding your awareness. Begin to pull your awareness back into the present moment. Notice how you are feeling right now.

You are not judging. You are not changing anything. Just noticing. Allow yourself to notice how you are feeling right now. Notice what is around you with all your senses.

Feel the breath in your nostrils. The touch of your clothes against your skin. Breathe deeply and smell the fresh scent in the air. Taste it. Listen to the sounds outside. Within the room. Outside the door.

Listen. Listen to the sounds of life and know that you are here now as part of that picture of life.

You are not alone. There are others who, even as they walk past your door, share this life with you. Yet they don't have to intrude upon your peace. You can choose to respond to them. Or not.

You can use your power to do anything you want and you can trust yourself.

So once again, take another deep breath and relax. Sink deeply into the peace of your inner self and concentrate on the power of imagination. Use your imagination to control the restlessness of your thoughts.

Imagine that at this moment you are by yourself and out at sea. Far, far from land.

Your everyday concerns feel restless in your mind but as the wind blows in your hair you feel its coolness soothing any anxieties and upsets. As you look at the water around you, you feel the stresses and difficulties of the day leaving you and floating across the choppiness of the waves away from you.

The wind starts to abate and a light breeze takes its place teasing the movement of the sea into sparkles of sunlight.

Gently follow your mind into the sea and feel the rippling water flowing over you. Can you feel it?

It is almost as if you are now standing in an underwater cavern, alone and at peace.

Beams of warming sunlight flicker across your eyes and the sea of your mind becomes calm and tranquil.

If you start to look around you, you will see that this underwater cavern is really a gallery of translucent mirrors.

See it rotating around you, as if moving slowly on a shimmering wheel.

You are watching the everlasting movement of the wheel of life.

This is your life. With you at the centre.

If you look closely you will find that each mirror reflects something from your past.

There are good memories there and bad ones.

Spend a little time now watching the moving images in this underground cave. A little time with those memories.

Don't be frightened of them for they are in the past. They cannot follow you into the present unless you decide they should be there.

You have the power of decision. Nobody else.

Listen to the rotation of the movement of the sea, and watch the cycle of all the different experiences in your life. But let it pass. No anxieties, no regrets.

Listen to the motion of the sea.

So this is your life. All the good things, all the bad, are really just a rotating mirror of events and circumstances that reflect back to us who we are and what we want. Moments and memories that serve to inspire or depress us, but they are only memories.

See the great wheel begin to fade and watch the glowing images on its surface recede with it.

See all the anxieties and regrets and let them go. Watch them dissolve into the misty secret shadows of the past. For they belong to another time. Their place is in the past but your life is continuing now. You live in the present.

Shed a tear if you must, but let it all go. Let it go. It belongs to another time.

The ponderous movement of the rotating mirrors glimmer and fade and you find yourself once again in the shimmering light of a great underwater cavern.

Shafts of sunlight flickering far above seem to draw you upwards and you find yourself rising up through the waves. As you surface you see a small boat rocking gently beside you on a translucent sea. Without effort you climb into it and lay back feeling the cool water upon your skin amidst the warming rays of a summer sun and listen for a moment to the steady lapping of waves around you.

This sea, these waves, can be likened to the ocean of your mind, your memories, your past. And the boat?

The little boat is your inner protection that, in spite of wind and storm, keeps you safe and secure. Bobbing and weaving lightly on its surface.

Put your hand down and feel the smoothness of the water. Feel the strength of that little boat around you in that ocean of dreams and be glad. Look up and you see the sun in a clear blue sky. Watch the birds fly effortlessly overhead. This world of magic is yours to make of what you will.

The present belongs to you. Only you. Just the same as your past. You are your own protector. You are your own person. You have your own power and that power is the energy of all life. You can trust yourself.

Say to yourself silently:

I am my own person. I have my own power. This is the first day of the rest of my life and from now on I will govern my own life.

It is time to return now. Draw yourself slowly back into your present surroundings. Listen to the sounds of the room and of those outside. As you listen to these sounds think of what you have seen. What you have learned from the experience and where you want to go from here.

It is often said that the place in which we live is not in the world of imagination but the reality of our life on earth. Yet, what you think and feel comes from your imagination and helps create your present life. You can live with your memories if you so choose but there is no need to live with any regrets. You can do whatever you want, whenever you want. You are your own protector and you can trust yourself. This is the first day of the rest of your life.

End of meditation

Allow yourself plenty of time to return to everyday consciousness once the meditation is complete. It is essential you **earth yourself** *after the meditation to prevent energy loss and ways to earth or ground self include eating and drinking.*

The Power of the Subconscious

The spiritual journey ascending the Tree of Life begins in Malkuth.

Malkuth starts the process off by encouraging us to **discriminate** and **de-clutter**.

It can be likened to **spiritual housework** and managing our lives more effectively.

Malkuth also gets us thinking about our **wants** and **needs**.

Have you considered your wants and needs?

Your needs are essential to your well-being and if they are not satisfied then this can affect your emotional foundation; your emotional stability.

Needs may change but you have to be aware of what they currently are.

Malkuth represents our physical body and the physical, material plane that we live in on Earth.

On its own the physical body is just a lump of meat – a dead weight, completely inanimate – it needs the life force, a personality, to bring it to life; to ensoul it.

The area we are going to look at now is the next level up, the level of **personality**. So we are going to move away from Malkuth and the physical body and explore the sephirah **Yesod** which is **sephirah** number **nine** and associated with the colour **violet**.

Everything has to go through this next area, **Yesod** – it is an extremely important factor. It is the **subconscious mind**.

So, how do we know when the subconscious is at work?

The **subconscious** is the whole bank of our **memory**.

Everything that has ever happened to us, not only in this present life but in all our past lives too, is stored in our subconscious and it can be triggered by events that we remember from the past.

We can find ourselves reacting to events: people: situations and not really understanding why, or the force of the reaction.

The main concentration of the Qabalah in the early stages is on the subconscious mind; trying to assess it and seeing how powerful it is in governing our life. What we are aiming for is to take conscious control of it as opposed to our subconscious controlling us.

It's about us **choosing** how we **react**.

To begin the process it often helps for us to first know the process of the mind.

Everyone has heard of the **conscious** and **subconscious** minds but there are two other kinds of minds.

There's the **higher mind** and the unconscious mind.

The unconscious mind is the mind that enables us to walk, sleep, breathe, blink and so on.

Completely unconscious motions.

Actions we perform without thinking about them govern this mind. They are totally unconscious.

We don't concentrate on the unconscious mind in the Qabalah because it is all part of the physical body but we are very interested in the other three minds: the conscious mind, subconscious mind and higher mind.

These three minds are situated in one big mind.

One way of trying to understand how it all works is to think of these three minds as if they were situated inside a long tunnel with the conscious mind at the entrance of the tunnel, the subconscious sitting in the middle and the higher mind at the far end.

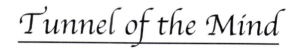

Tunnel of the Mind

Higher Mind
Memories of useful learning experiences

Subconscious Mind
Vast memory bank of information

Conscious Mind
Immediate events

It might help with the learning process to draw a tunnel on a piece of paper and enter where, within the tunnel, the conscious, subconscious and higher minds are situated.

The higher mind is also known as our **soul** mind, **superconscious** or **intuitive** mind.

Being able to access our higher minds or our intuition is what we are aiming to do because if we allow ourselves to be guided by our intuition then we will be far more able to make choices and decisions in our life that are right for us.

These are choices and decisions that are in line with our **Destiny**; that is – what we are destined to do this lifetime. **Fate** is what nudges us back onto the right path if we make decisions and choices that are out of line with our destiny.

More information on Fate and Destiny can be found in the Tiphareth workbook

If we can find a way of tuning into our intuition – our higher mind, then we can save ourselves time and pain.

To make the best use of our conscious, subconscious and higher minds – our thoughts need to be able to flow freely. There needs to be a free-flow of traffic moving from one end of the tunnel to the other, and back again.

In our **everyday lives** we are constantly using our **conscious minds**.

The **conscious mind** works with **immediate events** so it's the events that are happening **here** and **now**. Once these immediate events have occurred they sink directly into the memory bank of the subconscious. We can only remember so much information at any one time before those thoughts, that information, travels up the tunnel into the subconscious. All the memories are then stored within the subconscious.

The **subconscious** mind is like a **vast bucket of experience**. Every thought, feeling, emotion that you have ever had in this life and previous lives is contained here. It is a colossal memory bank of information that is sustained by you, so there is a difference in size between the two types of mind, between the conscious mind and subconscious.

If we want to remember something, if we relax our conscious minds, the information usually bobs to the surface of our subconscious where our conscious mind can easily access it. However, if we try to force ourselves to remember something, and wrack our brains but still can't remember, that's often because our conscious mind is too busy, too active trying to remember and the information can't get through.

You will probably have experienced for yourself when you have been trying to remember or recall something and quite often what happens is when you switch your conscious mind off the answer you are looking for suddenly pops into your head without any effort on your part.

The conscious mind is related directly to the brain and when we die, the physical body dies, the brain dies and so does the conscious mind.

However, all the memories of events that have occurred have sunk into the subconscious.

The higher mind takes out all the useful bits.

All the debris and unproductive emotions and all the things that cause stress and trauma are left in the subconscious.

The higher mind absorbs or filters out the useful bits from the subconscious and makes a separate entity of it which also travels with us from life to life.

So both the subconscious and higher minds travel with us from life to life.

The higher mind contains all the memories of the useful experiences of the past and puts aside the ones that it no longer needs, that are not necessary.

The idea is for us to become more aware of our attitude and the sort of information that is being fed into our subconscious mind via our conscious mind, and to consciously feed our conscious mind with good information that will go through the subconscious and then up to the higher mind. The higher mind can then directly absorb it and store it for us for when we need it later.

So, when we find ourselves with a problem, the chances are we have encountered a similar experience previously in either the present life or perhaps a past life and hopefully learnt something from it. That **learning**, stored in our **higher mind**, can then be sent down, through the subconscious mind, to be accessed by the conscious mind and applied in our everyday life.

That is called **acting on intuition**.

Sometimes we just **know something**.

It is not emotionally based, we just **know** – that is intuition.

Intuition is not the same as gut feeling. Gut feeling is emotionally based and unless we are incredibly strong on the emotional level it can be misleading.

Intuition is a **knowing** and it works from a **higher level**.

The job of the Qabalah is to try to get our conscious mind to absorb the subconscious and higher mind so they unite all as one. So that we are aware, all the time, of what our subconscious is doing, and also what the higher mind intends for us, and what information the higher mind has got for us that we might have forgotten, or cannot bring to the surface.

Because the subconscious travels with us from life to life it unfortunately means that we bring **excess baggage** through with us into present incarnations.

The subconscious is incredibly potent because it remembers everything and we can find ourselves reacting to something strongly in this life without really knowing why but we may be reacting to something that happened to us in a past life or **someone** from the past.

What tends to happen is a terrible experience occurs and the information or memory of that event sinks into the subconscious and stays there.

Human nature is such that it has a bad or frightening experience and hangs onto it.

The memory gets into the subconscious mind but cannot travel any further up to the higher mind because the subconscious has got hold of it with a vice-like grip. The memory then gets pushed right down into the subconscious.

Ideally what should happen is the experience and information of the event should **pass through the subconscious**, enabling the higher mind to extract the bits that are necessary, leaving the rest in the subconscious. The necessary or useful bits are the bits that have helped us **learn from that experience**.

Imagine a tunnel with traffic going in two directions. A fallen tree or jack-knifed lorry gets stuck in the middle and jams the way. This causes a massive blockage as the traffic can't move freely in either direction.

If you relate this to your own life, when you are in trauma you may be aware that someone is talking to you but you don't really hear them.

They are talking to you on a conscious level and you are trying to listen but you are so emotional you can't really take it in. You're not hearing.

When we are in trauma we can't think straight, so we can't rely on our intuition or our higher mind to send information through to help us because there's a blockage. This is the same as the scenario of the fallen tree or lorry blocking the tunnel, and preventing the free-flow of traffic.

All of our subconscious' are full of jack-knifing lorries. Some big, some smaller - all different sizes. All according to our experiences not only in this life but in other lives too.

The first step in the Qabalah is to find a clear channel through to our higher selves, our intuition.

We need a free-flow of thought traffic.

Whenever we have a problem the idea is for us to be able to silence the conscious mind and find a way of tapping into our higher selves, our intuition, to hear the answers that are there, waiting to help us, stored in our higher mind.

More on Silencing the Conscious Mind can also be found in the Binah Workbook.

Qabalah helps us by getting us to look at the state of our subconscious. To understand what trauma's or debris may be buried there affecting us, and to find ways of silencing our conscious minds. If our minds are constantly buzzing then we need to learn how to relax and clear all busy thoughts, and to find a clear passage-way through to our intuition.

If we can't turn off our conscious mind, and if we allow ourselves to be governed by our emotional reactions and responses, then our intuition or higher selves will have a hard job trying to reach us to help us make decisions and choices that are right for us.

When a memory buried within the subconscious gets triggered - this could be a memory from this life or a past life - that trigger sets off a reaction within us.

If we go through life reacting, reacting, reacting all the time and those reactions are unproductive then effectively we are not in control.

We are being controlled by our subconscious.

If we start to get to grips with the nature of us, understand how we think, know what our attitude is like, the sort of automatic habits we have got into, and recognise the sort of things that trigger us off then we are better equipped to handle situations, events and people in a way that is more productive and less destructive.

The Temple of Yesod

The Temple of Yesod is known as the **Treasure House of Images**.

This is where all our memories are – memories of our past lives.

The following is a meditation designed to help you experience this Temple of the Sea.

The journey will begin in Malkuth.

From Malkuth you will be lifted up through the astral waters to Yesod.

On your way you may see images of your past; images and memories of many lives and many dreams, images that belong to you and others too.

You may also feel strong arms around you, protecting you.

These could be the arms of your guide or sometimes **Atlas**, the **magical image** of **Yesod** - a beautiful naked man that is very strong and who holds up the rest of the Tree.

When you get to Yesod you will be introduced to the **Aishim** who are the **Angels** of **Yesod**.

The Aishim are the workers behind the scenes, manipulating and preparing the energy of Yesod to take shape and give birth on the Earth Plane.

Yesod – Temple of the Sea

We enter the temple of Malkuth with the sound of thunder in our ears.

As the door closes behind us we turn and see the triumphant flight of a great eagle, poised as if captured in a moment in time in the circular glass window above the great oak door.

The sound of rain abates and we look down, comforted by the warmth of the black and white tiles beneath our feet.

Somewhere in the distance we hear the haunting chorus of the Pilgrims, the seekers of Malkuth.

As we turn, and peer through the mist that seems to pervade our sight, we see them solemnly passing before us, ghostly intangible figures enshrouded in dark hooded cloaks of brown and grey.

A wind arises and the great bell echoes strangely in the temple. As we approach the altar in the eastern wall we feel a peculiar sense of imminence as if we are about to step into a world of dreams.

The dark double cubed altar glimmers with light as the central flame ducks and dives on its surface. And as we stand watching it in silent awe we suddenly become aware of a shadowy figure standing before us between the two mighty pillars of ebony and ivory.

Sandalphon smiles at us, his eyes aglow with life and as he moves his hands we see trails of sparkling energy spiralling from his fingers.

One by one he touches our forehead as if in greeting and **Paralda** swoops around us, the **King** of the element **air**.

As he darts, so he tugs at our clothes as he guides us through the two great pillars towards the three great oak doors at the back of the temple.

We look up and stare into the gentle eyes of a human face encircled in splinters of colour above the doors in the eastern wall and we wait poised in anticipation as Sandalphon approaches the central portal and turns towards us. He looks deep into our eyes and he tells us that we are about to enter the pathway to the temple of Yesod, the doorway to the subterranean subconscious and the idea of space.

It is the first bridge to the inner worlds of Light. He tells us not to fear for our guides and doorkeepers will meet us there and will raise us as if from the depths of a deep dark sea, cutting through the darkness of our memories beyond and up to the silver treasure house of images there.

Sandalphon turns and makes the sigil in the air before the central door, the sign of the pentagram.

Slowly the door creaks and opens and we step out into a swirling mist of violet light.

For a moment we feel bewildered and alone but then strong hands encircle us from behind and we find ourselves lifted in a cloud of protection up through the swirling sound.

> Allow yourself to move through the swirling current.

> Observe but do not fear the shadowy figures that pass you by.

They are images of your past, images and memories of many worlds and many dreams; images that belong to you and others too.

> Of all mankind.

Relax and allow your guides to help you move with the stream of consciousness, for you are part of it and you are protected.

You find yourselves swirling and circling, as you rise up and up through the darkness around you, spiralling towards some distant light far above.

Look up and you will see the light getting closer and closer now. It is as if you are surfacing from beneath a liquid pool, and the sun sparkles on the waters above.

You're rising up, away from the shadowy depths beneath, the subterranean world of space, the sea of the subconscious.

Your guide's arms are strong around you as they lift you now through the surface.

Allow them to lift you through the surface of the water, up, up .....

There, you can breathe freely now.

Feel the droplets of water falling from your hair. You have surfaced in a tranquil lagoon, sparkling with violet radiance. The atmosphere feels so light, filled with swirling sparks of darting brilliance, pulsing with life.

Watch those swooping towards and around in perfect formation.

These are the Aishim, the angelic force of Yesod, minute atom-like creatures each with a sun nucleus of fire and heat.

We glide easily to the edge of the lagoon feeling the cool water drip from our limbs as we climb out and sit with our guides for a moment at the edge of the crystal pool.

Our guide points and there in front of us we see a bridge spanning the waters to a temple.

There, it gleams in the far distance.

A pagoda, exquisite in structure, cut in mother of pearl with turrets of silver.

Our guide tells us that soon we must go inside. But first let us commune with them so that we may know something of the mysteries and perhaps we will see a glimpse of the Goddess of the Moon.

Our guide draws our attention now to what they say is the Moon Goddess who resides on the surface of the lagoon. They point to a glistening light in the centre and we see the bright reflection of a new moon rippling on the waters.

The moon we are told, takes on many phases.

Automatically we look up but there is nothing in the sky, just the gleaming eyes of the Aishim as they swirl in space around us.

Immediately a question arises in our minds but our guides put their fingers to their lips to silence our query and tell us that things are different here, that we must just watch and observe.

Reasoning is not the function of this sephirah.

It is just a mirror of events of Yesod and one day we will be able to discover the mysteries of all things and we will be able to understand.

The face of the moon on the waters glimmers and fades and we find ourselves rising with our guide and following them across the silver bridge towards the temple.

The luminous silver doors open before us as we and our guide walk into the temple of Yesod.

And there, to our joy we see the figure of the archangel Gabriel coming towards us.

A beautiful blue-green figure with silver flashes of light, and a tremendous swirl of colours of various shades of peacock tints shot with silver which are his wings and part of his extensive aura. It is as if he is surrounded in a cloud of sequinned stars, but we realise now that these are the Aishim, the angelic force of Yesod swirling around him. About his head and beneath his feet, streams of liquid silver ensue.

To our amazement we see him change into a tremendous pillar of silver light tinged with a mauve-grey aura reaching far into the dome of the temple and around this pillar again we see clouds of peacock blue and green.

Our guide smiles and tells us that this is Gabriel. This tremendous pillar should be conceived to be like a battery of the Universe, an electric battery. All actions of the Universe are switched, as it were, onto this great battery for this is the basis of vision and all astral sight.

Gabriel returns once again to his original form and smiles down at us, an all pervading love emanating from his aura.

We follow him through to the altar at the centre of the temple and for the first time we find ourselves looking around and seeing within. The great walls of the temple are made of silver, translucent and mirror-like in effect. We can see our reflections in them and if we look very carefully we can see also the reflection of our guide.

The temple floor is inlaid with tiles of deep blue, with images of the phases of the moon set around the floor in ebony and silver. There is a crescent-shaped pool spanned by a small bridge of mother of pearl exquisite in design.

The great domed ceiling over our heads is of deep blue as if reflecting a night sky, and there hanging, as if suspended in space, we see nine silver lamps over our heads.

The altar we see now before us is made of white marble and in its centre is a silver dish aglow with light. On the altar are nine silver goblets and we are told that we must drink from the waters of life from these goblets.

Gabriel lifts the mighty grail in his hands - aflood with light, and pours into each one of the silver cups. He turns, surrounded by the Aishim the little souls of fire, and invites us to drink our fill of the waters of life, the vital soul of existence.

And as we do so we catch a glimpse of the violet veil behind the altar, shot with silver, and hear the waters of the pool begin to bubble behind us.

For a moment we stand looking deep into its depths and Gabriel tells us that we and our guides must dive deep into its waters now on our journey back to the realms of Malkuth. He lays a gentle hand of farewell on our heads and we feel a surge of life enter our beings as if by magic.

We feel our guide take our hand and together we jump into the surging pool, deep into its depths and we are drawn down into its midst.

And once again, we find ourselves in Malkuth.

Sandalphon and the cherubim greet us now and all the elemental kingdoms come to join us in their joy of seeing us. Sandalphon turns and leads us to the central altar where we kneel before it and bid our farewell.

The sound of the pilgrims and the temple bell echoes in our ears and we know that we are once more worthy to join them. There is a little bit more we know, just a little bit more.

Spend this time now with Sandalphon and your guides and thank them for this experience for you have been honoured to enter the temple of Yesod.

Let the sound of the pilgrims now draw you into your normal surroundings.

You have been honoured by their presence but you are welcome.

End of Temple of Yesod

It is normal to receive information during each meditation. It is a good idea to make a log of everything you may get. Do not dismiss anything.

This record is useful to refer to and gradually as your awareness increases the Bigger Picture will begin to emerge and you may start to see a pattern.

Emotional Independence

Every temple offers a challenge and the challenge of Yesod is **Independence**.

Independence is known as the **virtue** of Yesod. The virtue is what we are aiming to aspire to.

This is emotional independence and means **not being controlled** by **subconscious triggers**. These are reactions and responses that we are not in control over. Something sets us off – something that the subconscious triggers.

Yesod draws our attention to the **way we emotionally react and respond** and helps us to learn how to become independent of subconscious reactions and to ignore outdated habits.

A habit is something we do automatically like biting fingernails and twiddling with hair.

Yesod can help us to break free from reacting in certain ways to certain situations or people. These habit patterns are automatic responses; reactions without thought.

The virtue (**Independence**) is what we are aiming to aspire to, whereas the vice (**Idleness**) is how we are more likely to behave or what trips us up and prevents us from achieving the virtue.

Idleness – this is about **not dealing with emotional issues**.

If our subconscious is full of memories of past events that we haven't let go of then the ripple effect may mean that on some level we are likely to be very reactive and emotional.

Remember, emotion isn't just about crying. Anger is also an emotion.

Each sephirah on the Tree of Life focuses on a different aspect within us.

The nature of Yesod tends to make us lethargic, so it is important we don't let emotional issues rule or drain us.

It is essential we understand the state of our subconscious and become aware of any debris or unfortunate memories that may be lurking there, potentially controlling or influencing our reactions.

Everything has to go through our subconscious

before it reaches us on a conscious level.

The State of our Subconscious

The subconscious is like a giant dustbin that contains all our experiences, all our memories.

It does not discriminate – it takes it all; soaks everything up whether we are consciously aware of it or not.

The **way** we emotionally react and respond to people, events and circumstances depends on:

- ✦ The **state** of our **subconscious**
- ✦ **Embedded memory patterns**

and how receptive we are to what our subconscious is trying to tell us.

Are you consciously aware of what pushes your buttons?

How do you receive messages sent to you from the subconscious - how reactive are you?

What is your **attitude** towards **past events** in your life? Do you think *that was then* and *this is now* or do you find yourself still trying to re-enact the past and re-living past events?

You may already be consciously aware of the answers to those questions but often we are not.

The way we react and respond is the result of a build-up of all that has gone before. Situations, events, people; all act as triggers. In some cases emotional reactions and responses have been brought through from past lives so we may have inherited factors to deal with and resolve.

Part of the challenge of Yesod is to clear blockages and get rid of memories that are not serving any useful purpose anymore.

We can begin the process of becoming aware of the state of our subconscious by taking note of the way we emotionally react and respond in certain situations and to people. We can re-programme our subconscious through *building positive images in our mind.

More on building positive images in the mind can be found in the Hod workbook.

If we are emotionally reacting all the time then not only will we be continually drained of energy and exhausted, but we will not be able to function properly in other ways or think straight either. To help with energy loss it is a good idea to ensure we keep our aura clean and prevent ourselves from being affected by outside influences.

One way to clean the aura is to take a shower. Water is a great purifier; it cleanses and washes away all the debris.

For more information on auras and healing see Tiphareth workbook.

Every sephirah holds a challenge. We have a **choice** in the **way** we **emotionally react** and **respond**. Blaming others for the way we react is not the way forward.

It is important we learn from the past. If we cling to resentments and emotionally react in ways that do not work then the chances are we are not **listening** to our higher self.

Acting on Intuition

Information to help us in present day situations can be found stored in our Higher Mind: our Intuition, or Soul Mind.

The Higher mind contains the answers to our questions however, in order for that useful information to filter through into our conscious mind and into conscious awareness, it has to go through our subconscious. We have to put ourselves in a **receptive** frame of mind to **hear** the answers.

We may have had similar experiences ourselves or watched others when emotionally they are *all over the place* and when you try to offer help they cannot hear you; they are not receptive or, everything you suggest – they have a reason why it won't work.

If our subconscious is stuffed full of anxieties, fears and prejudices then there is no clear way for information from the Higher Mind to pass through.

The answers to our problems remain out of our reach.

We have to actively find ways to relax and let go of attitudes, thoughts and worries that are blocking the subconscious and cluttering our conscious minds.

The sephirah Malkuth deals with de-cluttering and discriminating how you manage time, money and energy.

The vice of Malkuth is inertia – that means not taking action in your everyday life. The vice of Yesod is **idleness** – this is not the same as inertia. Idleness is about not being bothered to deal with negative habit patterns or thinking you don't need to do anything because it's not your problem.

*If you are reacting in a non-productive manner – **it is your problem**!*

*If you are caught in a negative cycle – **it is your problem**!*

There is an unwritten law within The Order of the White Lion which is:

Only repeat something 3 times.

After that you have to accept the person is not ready or does not want to hear. To keep going is a waste of energy and can be draining.

Another way we can find answers to help us is through our **Spirit Guides**.

Re-Incarnation

Do you consider we can experience everything life has to offer all in one lifetime?

Reincarnation works on the idea that life is a series of births and deaths, and those that die carry on living.

How do we know this is what happens?

Do you believe that those who have died can be of any use to us?

If so, how?

Astral Worlds & Spirit Guides

One of the first things taught within the Qabalah is the importance of de-cluttering our lives (Malkuth). We are encouraged to get our lives in order and to get rid of everything that has outlived its usefulness including attitudes that do not work for us.

The **clearing out** process is to help us make room for new, better things but also, it's to encourage spiritual energy to enter our lives.

The Tree of Life not only works on a personal, individual level it also operates on a universal level encompassing the **Bigger Picture**.

As well as focusing on our emotional foundation and subconscious, the sephirah **Yesod** also links us with the **Astral Worlds**.

As human beings we live in the physical plane of dense matter (Malkuth/Earth) and use our senses: **touch, taste, sight, smell** and **sound** as a means of surviving.

Yesod is the plane directly above and represents the **lower** Astral level.

The Astral Worlds and above operate at a higher vibration; a higher frequency than us on the Earth plane. The higher we move up the Tree of Life into the spiritual realms, the lighter the energy and more subtle and less tangible it becomes.

Although many people are unaware of this higher frequency or vibration it's no different really from humans not being able to hear the high pitch of a dog whistle. The sound of the whistle exists, because a dog can hear it, but it's out of most human's range of hearing.

The Astral Worlds are all around us and some people can see it. However, even though most people are unable to see the Astral Worlds or other spirit beings they can often **feel** its presence and **sense** astral beings. We can become more aware of their existence through using any of our senses.

When we die we move over to what is called a **local Astral World.**

We still retain our personalities. We don't suddenly have the answers to the universe, but we are able to see the **Bigger Picture** and we are able to impress the living with thoughts.

Spirit Beings are attracted to those who operate on a steady and harmonious level, and more stable emotional state of being. Everyone can experience a connection with spiritual energy.

If you ask for help they will respond. By meditating, getting our lives in order and living in a calm, balanced way we can easier connect with them and feel their presence.

These Beings can have a tremendous affect on us as individuals. They can help us by instilling a thought in our mind. The more we commune with them the closer they will feel to us and the distance between their world and ours will be less detached and easier to experience.

In the same way we can tune into other people's thoughts without any words being exchanged so Astral Beings can impress certain thoughts upon us that can affect us in the way we behave, and so on.

Have you had much experience with Spirit Guides?

Because we have the gift of **Free Will**, Guides cannot interfere without being asked for help.

Personal Spirit Guides

You may, or may not, be aware that you have your own personal guide that stays with you all the time.

When we are born we each have a guide who is committed to remain with us throughout our life as our own personal guide.

These personal guides are not there to protect us, they are there to guide us.

They can help us by instilling a *thought* in our mind or giving us what we may call a **premonition**.

Have you ever experienced getting a premonition about something that may have either encouraged you to do, or not do, something or told you in advance that something might happen?

The gift of **Free Will** means guides are not allowed to intervene unless we request their help. They are not allowed to do anything except by our own permission and if we don't believe in them then we are not going to ask anything of them, which is quite sad.

Guides can oversee us, they can stand guard over us, they can try to impress us with thoughts but unless we specifically ask them they cannot help. One of the difficulties of being a personal guide is the fact that they are often ignored, and they might be there, with you.

When we do spiritual work not only will we have our guide with us but many others from the Astral Worlds may nosy in as well because they are interested in helping us.

Our personal guide is with us all the time. Some people get a shivering feeling and that's how they know they are around. Others get thoughts coming into their head and see them. Some people feel a tingling over their face or arms, or a buzzing sensation in their ears. It can be anything but the point is, it's **very significant to you**.

If you want to explore further then start to become aware of certain things, certain feelings and if those feelings repeat themselves then put out a thought in your mind and say: **OK, I connect with you, can you make it a bit more apparent please?**

The most common sensation is a tingling somewhere on the body usually the face. **You need to actively** try to make a connection. Try to connect for yourself and ask them to be more specific if you are not sure.

You may not know what they look like or know their name or anything but if you make a request and ask them to make themselves known to you they will, but they won't if you are frightened. They are not there to terrorise you. They are there to help but if they sense they will frighten the living daylights out of you by making themselves known, then they won't!

What they may do instead is make some sort of signal that will constantly come to your attention. It could be a dripping tap or a light flickering on and off. So, put your own testers on it and if you think you've got the signal or their means of trying to attract your attention then ask them to do it again.

It can just be a **feeling**.

When we do any sort of visualisation work our guide usually stands behind us and is there to nurture, guide and emotionally support us.

Sometimes high-powered, more evolved guides will move in to help us, particularly through transitional phases of our life. They are usually from a higher level. It is very hard for high-powered guides to stay with us for a lifetime because for them the earth plane energy is very dense and it's like walking through concrete!

Like attracts like, and we normally have someone of our own level of evolvement and development guiding us for our lifetime. Unlike us they don't get put off by the way we behave, and they will never leave us. They have a much wider over-view of things than we do.

We have a worm's eye-view.

They see the bigger picture because they have a greater understanding of the circumstances. They are still personalities but they don't get so involved in personality issues like we do and are more likely to laugh than get fed-up because they can see more.

Our personal guide can bring a feeling of comfort around us and generally will work on personality issues. They are not interested in world affairs. It is not their job or place to get into that, but if it's part of your future role to get involved in humanitarian affairs then you will have higher guides who will come in and help as well. And, if you are very distraught over an emotional, personality issue but your welfare is really important for a future humanitarian concern then you would get higher-powered guides moving in to help.

Our guide is with us all the time and when we're happy, we're happy but when we're miserable and life isn't great then that's when we're more likely to be sensitive to their presence and vibration, because we are actively searching for support and answers.

Other guides move in and out according to what help, guidance and support we need so if you suddenly find you have an immense healing ability it is invariably because *another* guide - *not* your personal guide, has moved in to help you with that. Sometimes temporary guides move in to help three or four people at once which explains why you may think you have a particular guide only to find someone else has them too.

These temporary guides are not to remain with you all the time. They move in and out, and help different people at different times according to what tuition they need.

More information on Spirit Guides can be found in the main OWL website.

Memory

Memory is another aspect of Yesod. Yesod can help us to recognise and let go of unfortunate memories that hold us back and affect our emotional stability.

An unstable emotional foundation not only ties us to the past but it can affect our ability to recall information that might be useful for us to remember. Attitudes, negative thoughts and worries block the subconscious and clog up the conscious mind making it very difficult for information to get through.

If you have problems trying to recall information, instead of wracking your brain, try relaxing – you may surprise yourself when the answer pops into your conscious mind without you even trying.

Our memories are perfect – the problem we have in recalling information is often to do with our inability to allow it to float to the surface of our conscious mind. We need to learn how to relax the conscious mind to allow the thoughts to flow freely.

The experience of Yesod is very much to do with looking at the strength of our emotional foundation.

Memories can easily become distorted if we are not emotionally in balance.

The next section, the **Spirit of Yesod**, looks at how you can understand more about the energy of this sephirah.

The Spirit of Yesod

Astrologically the moon aligns itself to Yesod on the Tree of Life and the **mirror** is a symbol associated with this sephirah. The moon acts as a mirror in that the light from the sun bounces off the moon and what we see on earth is but a reflection of the sun's radiant energy.

How much light the moon reflects during the night is dependent on its cycles.

During a new moon phase, the moon is barely visible in the night-sky as it is positioned between the sun and earth.

The side of the moon that is lit up by the sun during this time is facing away from earth. The effect of the sun and moon as they move together like this means strong gravitational forces are felt on earth through the tides. As well as understanding how the tides can be affected it is also important to know that as much as 75% of the body weight of a new-born baby is made up of water.

That percentage gradually decreases from birth to old age. For an adult male approximately 60% of his body weight is made up of water. That's still a large percentage. So if the effects of the moon influence earth's tides – perhaps we shouldn't be surprised if we too feel its effects and respond accordingly.

When the moon is full, the Sun and Moon are pulling in opposite directions and it is during this time that high tides occur. It is also during this potent time that emotions can run high as people feel (albeit on a subconscious level) the impact of this **tug of war**.

We can get into the Spirit of Yesod by becoming more aware of the phases of the moon. We may find life works better for us if we appreciate and work with these lunar cycles:

- A **new moon** is a good time for new beginnings. We may, during a new moon phase almost feel compelled to take action. This phase would be a good time to travel during the hours of night without being seen.

- During the **first quarter** phase the waxing moon appears to **grow** in the night-sky and at the same time we may feel like we are **building up** to something and the pressure is on. This fertile period can be quite a testing time but seeds that germinate during a rising or waxing moon quite often get a head start over others.

- The **full moon** follows 14 or 15 days after a new moon. The full moon gives out the most light; the whole of the moon can be seen in the night-sky as it reflects the maximum light from the sun. This is when the moon's energy is at its most potent and full of magical power. This is a time of plenty, of ripening and completeness. It is also an awareness phase; a good opportunity for gaining enlightenment and clarification

- ✦ The **waning** phase is when the moon starts to decrease in size. This is not the best time to start something new. Everything has come to a head; the energy of the moon is now ready to wind down. This is a time to tie up loose ends, wrap up old projects, and reflect on all that has gone before. It is a time for gathering all that experience in preparation for the next, new wave of energy; the new phase yet to come. The **dark** phase is a resting time to relax and do nothing.

Much information can be found through the study of astrology. The **moon** gives us insights into how we **emotionally react** and **respond**, and the sign of the zodiac the moon is positioned in at the time of birth can help us understand why we react and respond in the way we do.

More information Astrology can be found on the OWL website

Experiencing Yesod

The following idea is one way you can immerse yourself in the Yesod Experience.

One of the major symbols associated with Yesod is the **mirror**.

When looking in a mirror we must try to remember not to take what we see literally.

As an exercise hold your arms outstretched and lay a large mirror on top.

You can look into a mirror at different angles and see different things reflected back.

Try walking around a room or a house being guided only by the reflection in the mirror, as you look **down** into it!

Is this something you find easy to do or challenging?

Do you keep bumping into things?

Each sephirah focuses on a different type of energy and some sephiroth are going to affect us greater than others. It is important to note your reaction as you experience these different energies.

A driver will use a car mirror to see other cars when driving.

Sometimes though, there are blind spots so we mustn't always take what we see literally.

Yesod deals in stories with underlying meanings as well as literal ones.

Yesod is not about telling lies but more about reflecting the truth according to our level of comprehension in the hope that we may understand.

Another useful exercise to help in our understanding of Yesod is to spend some time by the sea or near water.

Yesod is the temple of the sea and the element water within us aligns with our feelings, emotions and love.

We can also access our subconscious through our dreams.

What sort of dreams do you have?

Each sephirah, as well as having a vice, virtue and archangel assigned to it also has other information pertaining to the experience of that sephirah/temple.

On the next page is a list of correspondences to **Yesod** – the **Foundation**, including symbols that relate and which, if you pick up on any of them during meditations or in your conscious, waking life, can be linked to this particular sephirah and temple.

YESOD – The Foundation

Magical Image:	A beautiful naked man, very strong
Name of Power:	Shaddai El Chai; Almighty Living One
Archangel:	Gabriel
Angels:	Aishim; the Souls of Fire
Planetary Attribution:	The Moon
Virtue:	Independence (emotional)
Vice:	Idleness (thinking you haven't got to do anything or can't be bothered)
Spiritual Experience:	Vision of the Machinery of the Universe
Titles:	Treasure-house of Images; the Sphere of Illusion
Symbols:	The perfumes and the sandals; the mirror
Deities (Gods):	All Moon Deities: Goda, Diana, Thoth, Ganesha, Hecate, Sin
Precious Stone:	Quartz
Plant:	Willow, Mandrake
Perfume:	Jasmine, Ginseng, all fragrant roots
Animal:	Elephant, tortoise, toad

Reasons to use temple of Yesod:

- ✦ Worries over the reactive process – past or present subconscious memories
- ✦ Meeting guides
- ✦ Looking at past lives

NO REGRETS

Recording events and personal responses can be invaluable for future reference.

*If at first you don't seem to see much in the meditation, don't worry. This will likely improve as you go on. Concentrate on what you **do** get rather than what you don't and give yourself plenty of time to peruse on it. It is often surprising what you can glean from a seemingly duff meditation.*

1) Mood beforehand:

2) Landscape by the sea:

3) How were the waves? Choppy or calm?

4) Mirrors:

5) What reflections of your past did you see?

6) Memories:

7) Anxieties and regrets:

8) How easy/hard was it to let go?

9) Message / symbolism:

10) Overall learning from meditation:

YESOD CONSOLIDATION

Each sephirah on the Tree of Life invites us to look at different aspects within ourselves. Yesod encourages us to explore the state of our subconscious and discover how our memories of the past continue to affect us.

The power of the subconscious is awesome and for most of us, beyond our control. Every single thing that has ever happened, not only in this life, but in all our past lives too, is stored within its vast memory banks. How affected we are by these memories is reflected in the way we handle everyday events and those around us. The challenges of Yesod provide us with the opportunity to reassess the way we respond in our everyday life and to remain in control over our emotional reactions.

Uncontrolled emotion is uncontrolled energy and non-productive. It can be damaging, not only to ourselves but to others also that are caught up in its chaos.

What we are aiming for with Yesod is to become independent over our emotions; this is *not about suppressing* but about being able to handle them.

It's very simple really. If the way we react and respond brings the sort of results we are looking for then all is well. However, if our reactions and responses are non-productive then effectively we are handing over our power and our subconscious is in control – not us.

Yesod can help us to identify negative patterns of behaviour that have become ingrained in us like a bad habit. How we behave is linked to how emotionally stable we are.

Astrology can be an extremely useful tool in helping us to get to **Know Thyself**. The way we see Our Self may be very different from how others see us and becoming aware of the sort of energies we are drawing towards ourselves can be very helpful if we want to change the pattern.

All the other sephiroth on the Tree of Life have to go through Yesod to reach us on a physical level (Malkuth) on the Earth plane. If our subconscious is packed full of unfortunate memories holding us back and our emotional foundation is unstable, then it becomes extremely difficult for those higher energies to filter through.

Our guides will not be able to impress us with thoughts and images if we are not in receptive mode, and information stored in our higher minds (our intuition) that could help us to manage our lives more effectively will not be able to reach us unless we consciously make the effort to switch off our busy conscious minds to hear the answers that lie within.

A key phrase throughout the Qabalah is **Know Thyself**.

The journey up the Tree of Life begins on the ground floor and then moves into the realms of the personality.

The way we behave relates to Malkuth: Action in Manifestation.

The **trigger** that encourages that behaviour comes from **Yesod**, the emotional foundation.

Knowing Thyself includes knowing where strengths and weaknesses lie within the personality. It is knowing what is potentially going to push your buttons and when you are likely to hand over your power by responding and behaving in an unproductive manner.

When something or someone pushes your buttons and you **cease to react**, and instead remain indifferent,

then,

you are **emotionally independent** and in **control**.

Worlds Apart

Written by Jenni Shell, founder of the Mystery School of Maat and The Order of the White Lion, this book describes the motivation behind her life's work. Available in paperback, Kindle and iBooks formats.

In this highly inspiring factual account, Jenni Shell traces the circumstances and consequences of traumatic events in two early childhoods: the one of her mother in the Edwardian era, and her own in the last years of the Second World War and after.

Although her mother had been diagnosed with a form of schizophrenia, there were indications that she might have been silenced, and it became her daughter's heartfelt commitment to bring to light the 'truth' about what might have been a tragic misdiagnosis.

Trying to understand her mother's suffering led the young woman to discover spiritual meaning in many so-called 'delusional' realities and synchronicities, which seemed to contradict her traditional upbringing. We become witness to a life-long search in an attempt to reconcile reason, practicalities and the soul's cosmic way of communication, and how this experience led her into mediating and teaching what she had learnt to many others.

Worlds Apart is, in a personal sense, a late and moving story of redemption: an account of the never told events that triggered her mother's illness, and ultimately the path of healing commenced in the next generation.

In 1981 Jenni founded Maat – a Qabalah or mystery school designed to inspire individuals to put into practice their life as personality, soul and spirit, beyond any rigid perspective. Well over 6,000 people from all walks of life attended, and have had the chance to work closely with this powerful, down to earth and modest teacher.

Despite her exposure to the public, Jenni has not sought a great deal of public attention. Worlds Apart shows why. Her whole life's focus - initially triggered by family trauma – has always remained in exploring the fine line between what can be misunderstood as mental illness on the one hand, and the urgent language of spiritual impressions on the other. Students felt attracted to and deeply understood by this approach.

The need to understand the vital forces of the psyche and adjust one's life practically in order to grow as a human being, has always been at the centre of her life and teachings.

Visit www.orderofthewhitelion.com for more information and where to buy.

Tree of Life workbooks in the series

© Copyright Jenni Shell and Lorraine Morgan

The following workbooks are step by step guides, designed for beginners to aid the student on their journey of self discovery exploring the Qabalistic Tree of Life.

As in all things, a good place to start is at the beginning and the sephirah of the Earth Plane:

- **Malkuth** - The **Kingdom**

When studying the Qabalah we often start off at the bottom of the Tree of Life, and begin by familiarising ourselves with the sephirah of the Earth Plane known as The Kingdom. The Hebrew name for this sephirah is Malkuth. Malkuth represents the physical plane - the world we live in, and the way we handle the energy of the material world. We would look to the Temple of Malkuth to help us find answers if we are having problems keeping ourselves grounded; experiencing challenging issues around money, or if we want to find solace and peace to enable us to re-coup lost energy.

- **Yesod** - The **Foundation**

The temple of Yesod is a beautiful sea temple. This sephirah focuses on the power of our subconscious; our emotional foundation and emotional stability. Yesod also links us to the Astral Worlds and Spirit Guides. We would look to the Temple of Yesod for help with the responsive process; handling emotional reactions; connecting with our personal guides, and accessing past life information.

- **Hod** - **Splendour** of the **Mind**

The sephirah Hod focuses on our Attitude and the power of Thought. Here we explore the Tunnel of the Mind and become more consciously aware of the sort of images we build in our mind. We would look to the Ice temple of Hod to help us to examine our attitude, and change any images that may be negative to our growth. Hod also helps us to build positive imagery eg. Magical Images; to form commitments, and to find the real truth of our thoughts.

- **Netzach - Victory** over **Feelings**

The teachings of Netzach help us to gain Victory over our Feelings and lift ourselves out of the restrictions of the personality, helping us to raise to the level of the soul - the sephirah Tiphareth. Netzach acts as a springboard to the upper part of the Tree, but first we have to become aware of how we really feel, and explore our attitude towards relationships - including the relationship we have with Self. Netzach helps us to discover the true nature of who we really are; the magic that lies hidden within just waiting to be brought to life. We would look to the Emerald temple of Netzach for creative inspiration; to help us deal with polarity and relationship issues, and to connect with the magical energy of the rawness of nature.

- **Tiphareth - Devotion to the Great Work**

The sephirah Tiphareth takes us into the realms of the Soul where we get the opportunity to connect and commune with the soul and higher more evolved guides. The virtue of Tiphareth is Devotion to the Great Work and it is important for us to remember that if we wish to pursue spiritual work and be of service in some way to others we must be prepared to work on ourselves, and help our Self rise above the level of the personality when times are challenging. Tiphareth helps us to heal ourselves so we may remain balanced and in harmony no matter what is happening in our everyday lives.

- **Geburah - Vision of Power**

In Geburah we become aware of mightier forces and begin to understand the role of the Soul, and the purpose of Karma. The challenges we face in this life are linked to our past lives. Geburah helps to expose traits within our personality that bind us to the continuous cycle of birth, death and rebirth, and reveals the links we share with others.

It is in Geburah that we experience the Will of the Soul.

- **Chesed - Mercy**

Chesed is where the journey really begins. **Part One of Chesed** takes us in Search of the Truth. Here we explore the Bigger Picture and attempt to strengthen our connection with the Teachers of Humanity - evolved Masters who can teach us how to walk in Time with the natural order of the Universe thus drawing us nearer to finding peace for the soul.

In **Workbook Two** we learn about the Evolution of Flame and the first wave of creation. This workbook raises our awareness of the role the angels and archangels play in the bigger picture, and how they can help us on our journey to enlightenment. In the Temple of Chesed we may catch a glimpse of the part we play in the grand scheme of Life, and find out how we too may be of service to others - just as the Masters, who have walked this journey before us, have been in service to us.

- **Binah - Understanding**

Binah represents the Womb of Creation and Mother of Form.

In this sephirah, at the top of the black pillar of Form, we explore the Principles of Sound and learn how to Silence the Conscious Mind to hear the call of the Spiritual Mother who watches over her children.

Binah is Aima - the bright, fertile Mother of Creation and Ama - the dark, sterile Mother of the Underworld.

It is in Binah that we examine the roots of our Faith and look deeper into the Four Worlds and extended Tree of Life.

- **Chokmah Soul Functions**

In Chokmah we explore the force of our Creative Power and decide how we can be of Service to Humanity. This Workbook is an Introduction to Soul Functions and can be used in conjunction with the Chokmah Workbooks. Most people are unaware of their Soul Functions or how to perform them in everyday life. To realise our full potential we need to know how to direct our creative power. The Soul Function Workbook explains in more detail what the functions mean and how to recognise them.

- **Chokmah - Wisdom**

Chokmah is the sephirah of Freedom and Spiritual Truths. It is the sephirah that aligns with the Will of the Spirit and Spiritual Direction. In this region of the Tree of Life the aim is to contact our creative power, and bring it down to earth.

In **Chokmah Workbook One** we explore how we use the senses and how we can further stimulate and balance the two hemispheres of the brain to spark the sixth sense (intuition) and third eye into action.

Chokmah is also the sephirah of Wisdom.

In **Chokmah Workbook Two** the emphasis is on Divine Wisdom and looking at ways to enter inner worlds of existence. This helps us to develop our psychic ability, and gain insights pertaining to the destiny and spiritual direction of the whole of humanity.

- **Kether** - the **Crown**

Situated at the top of the Tree of Life on the middle pillar of equilibrium, Kether represents Spiritual Perfection. At this level we are dealing with the intangible. Therefore, as with all the previous sephiroth in this series of workbooks, the approach to Kether is a practical one. In this workbook we attempt to see through the veil of our earthly perceptions. We explore the existence of other dimensions and try to connect with more advanced energies, and - by using an Inner Spirit Meditation - enter the dwelling place of our spirit.

The Archangels (Meditation)

The Archangels meditation has been developed with protection in mind.

Specially produced these mighty archetypes, and their kingdoms, increase so powerfully in imagery that, maybe for you, they will become fully alive?

Instructions for this meditation:

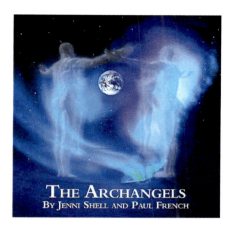

1. Choose a crystal and hold it in your hand

2. Sit in a comfortable position facing East

3. Close your eyes, start the CD and visualise

4. Once you have listened to this CD you will have 'programmed' the crystal you are holding, and each time you touch this crystal it will automatically put the protection of the archangels around you

The Story

Ancient man, whilst studying the nature of existence, discovered that the four mighty elements which governed life were fundamental to all manifestation. These elements are: Air Fire Water and Earth. Understanding themselves as part of manifestation these ancient people searched for the elements within themselves.

As their thoughts were free moving, and unseen, they likened them to the element Air.

As their desires burned in their breasts so they likened this to the element Fire.

As tears flowed in response to their feelings so they likened this to the element Water.

And, as the stability of their bodies, like the planet they lived upon, was the basis of survival, so this then represented the element Earth.

Extending this understanding it was thus determined that there were four inner requirements for lasting happiness. They were:

    Peace of Mind - Air / Thoughts

    Courage of Convictions - Fire / Desires

    Love within the Heart - Water / Feelings

Strength of Resolve - Earth / Stability

Just as the four elements are the building bricks of manifestation so these four great truths became the building bricks of civilisation and were eventually known as the attributes of Faith, Hope, Charity and Understanding.

We hear of these qualities in Spiritual teachings but few people really appreciate their meaning or the history behind them. In ancient times the wise men of the Aztecs, Shamen, Israelites, Egyptians and many others, including the Massai Tribes of Africa, lived by these beliefs, and throughout the ages pieced together pictorial images which described the four great concepts in a way that all could visualise and understand. Over aeons of time these images were continuously built by man and ensouled by spiritual forces until eventually they became accepted by all the religions of the world as archetypes of great power, described by different names but with the same faces. In Western tradition the archetypes are known as the Archangels: Raphael, Mikael, Gabriel and Uriel. These angelic forces represent respectively:

Peace through Faith - Raphael

Courage through Hope - Mikael

Love through Charity - Gabriel

Strength through Understanding - Uriel

The Archangels meditation is available to purchase from The Order of the White Lion website.

www.orderofthewhitelion.com

Qabalah (Kabbalah)

Qabalah is an ancient philosophy of life that takes us on a journey of self-discovery and greater awareness of the bigger spiritual picture, and the role we each play within it.

The teachings are 'mapped out' on the Qabalistic Tree of Life.

Qabalah is not a religion - it is more a way of life, and although it does not claim to prevent life's challenges, it does help us to understand why situations may occur and show us how to make life better. Its value is in the use of the Tree of Life.

The Tree of Life is a beautifully simple psychological and spiritual tool that reveals inspirational insights empowering individuals to expand their thinking and improve their life.

The Order of the White Lion and Isis Qabalah Tuition are run by ordinary people who, for many years, have studied the art of Self-understanding.

Through our series of practical workbooks we aim to inspire others to explore and activate creative energy, and find productive ways to channel it for the benefit of all.

There is so much in life for us to experience, and take part in. This series of workbooks help prepare us for the journey, and to be ready, open and receptive for what may lay ahead ……..

www.orderofthewhitelion.com

www.isisqabalahtuition.com

© Copyright Jenni Shell and Lorraine Morgan 2008 all rights reserved.

These workbooks are compiled and written with the utmost integrity and concentration on correct procedures. However, it is essential that they be regarded as information only.

In no event will the authors, or OWL/Isis websites, be liable for any consequences of the use of these workbooks, and therefore any action taken, or reliance placed on the information given, is entirely at your own risk.

Made in the USA
Coppell, TX
21 March 2022

75307964R00033